THE OFFICIAL
MANCHESTER
UNITED
ANNUAL 2000

WRITTEN AND COMPILED BY CLIVE DICKINSON
WITH ILLUSTRATIONS BY DAVID FARRIS

£6.25
UK ONLY

First published in 1999 by Manchester United Books
André Deutsch Ltd, 76 Dean Street, London, W1V 5HA

www.vci.co.uk

Text copyright © 1999 Manchester United Books
Illustrations copyright © 1999 André Deutsch Ltd
Photographs copyright © 1999 John Peters
Pictures for The World of Manchester United sourced
from Leonardo MediaBank: www.leonardo.com
Thanks to Luke Chester, Jack Stalker and Max Jones for their Fantastic Art

A catalogue record for this title is available from the British Library

ISBN 0 233 99527 7

Design by Traffika Publishing Ltd.
Front cover lenticular image produced by OpSec International Plc.
Illustrations by David Farris

Reprographics by Digicol and Printing by Jarrold Book Printing, England

CONTENTS

OFF TO THE MATCH

All the words listed below are related to watching a home match. They can all be found in the grid opposite, reading up, down, across or diagonally, in either direction. Use a pencil and a ruler to help you find them. When you have traced out all the words, the left-over letters (starting and ending with an X) and reading from left to right down the grid, spell out a message about your favourite ground.

CHEER
CORNER FLAG
FINAL WHISTLE (2 LINES)
FLOODLIGHTS
GOAL
HALF TIME (2 LINES)
HOME TEAM
HOT PIES (2 LINES)
KICK-OFF (2 LINES)
MANCHESTER
MATCH
NORTH STAND (2 LINES)
PLAYERS
PENALTY AREA
SCORING
SCARF-WAVING (2 LINES)
SEAT
SHOT
STADIUM
TICKETS
TURNSTILE
VISITORS

UNITED AT HOME

Andy Cole
Man Utd v Derby County

Dwight Yorke
Man Utd v Chelsea

Paul Scholes
Man Utd v Newcastle Utd

Denis Irwin
Man Utd v Newcastle Utd

Dwight Yorke
Man Utd v Fulham

Nicky Butt
Man Utd v Notts Forest

Ryan Giggs
Man Utd v LKS Lodz

David Beckham
Man Utd v Charlton Athletic

Jaap Stam
Man Utd v Liverpool

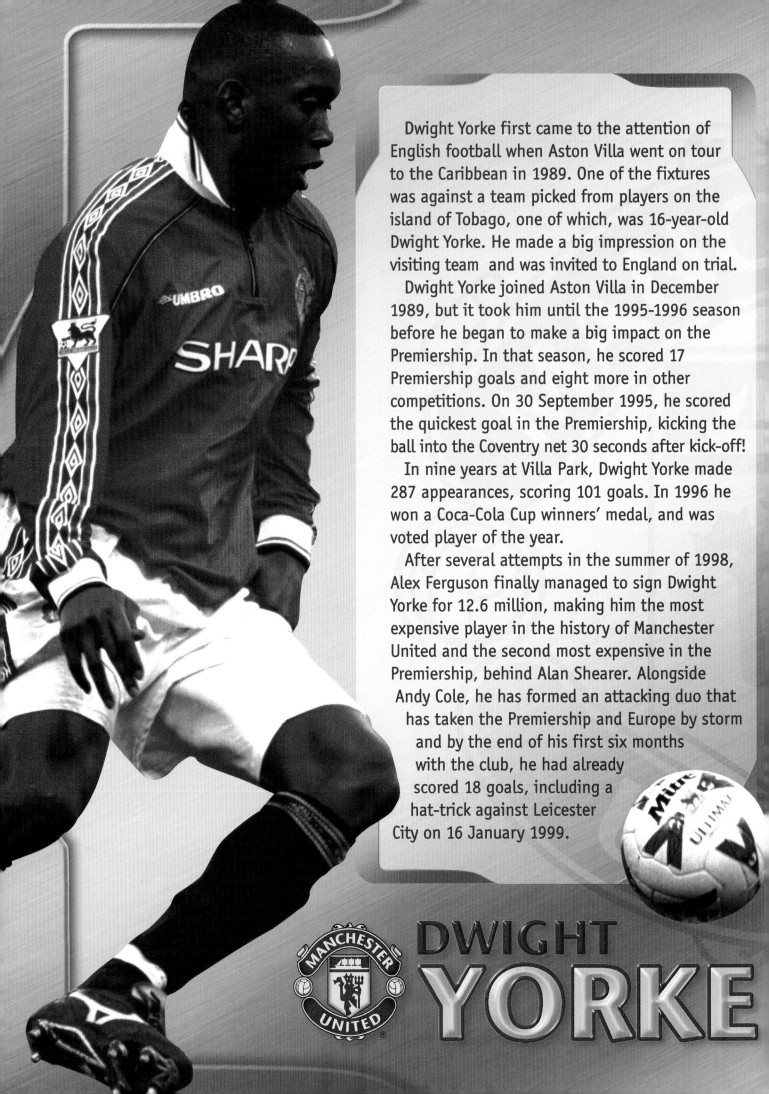

Dwight Yorke first came to the attention of English football when Aston Villa went on tour to the Caribbean in 1989. One of the fixtures was against a team picked from players on the island of Tobago, one of which, was 16-year-old Dwight Yorke. He made a big impression on the visiting team and was invited to England on trial.

Dwight Yorke joined Aston Villa in December 1989, but it took him until the 1995-1996 season before he began to make a big impact on the Premiership. In that season, he scored 17 Premiership goals and eight more in other competitions. On 30 September 1995, he scored the quickest goal in the Premiership, kicking the ball into the Coventry net 30 seconds after kick-off!

In nine years at Villa Park, Dwight Yorke made 287 appearances, scoring 101 goals. In 1996 he won a Coca-Cola Cup winners' medal, and was voted player of the year.

After several attempts in the summer of 1998, Alex Ferguson finally managed to sign Dwight Yorke for 12.6 million, making him the most expensive player in the history of Manchester United and the second most expensive in the Premiership, behind Alan Shearer. Alongside Andy Cole, he has formed an attacking duo that has taken the Premiership and Europe by storm and by the end of his first six months with the club, he had already scored 18 goals, including a hat-trick against Leicester City on 16 January 1999.

DWIGHT YORKE

JAAP STAM

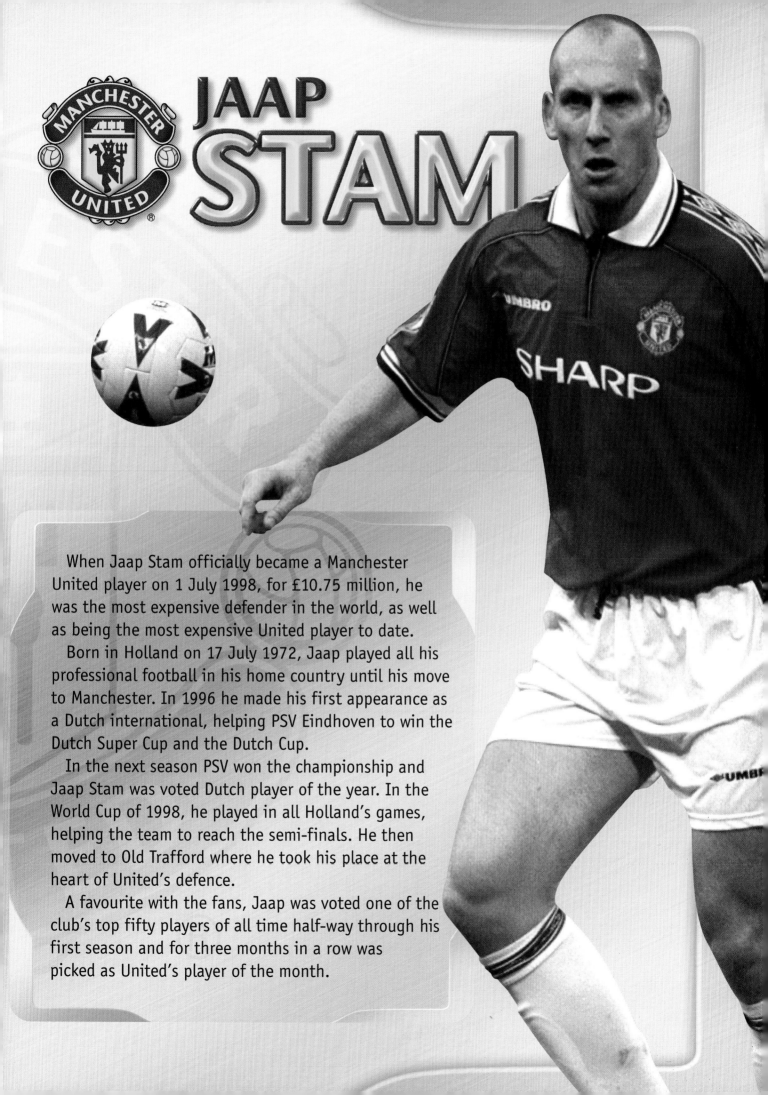

When Jaap Stam officially became a Manchester United player on 1 July 1998, for £10.75 million, he was the most expensive defender in the world, as well as being the most expensive United player to date.

Born in Holland on 17 July 1972, Jaap played all his professional football in his home country until his move to Manchester. In 1996 he made his first appearance as a Dutch international, helping PSV Eindhoven to win the Dutch Super Cup and the Dutch Cup.

In the next season PSV won the championship and Jaap Stam was voted Dutch player of the year. In the World Cup of 1998, he played in all Holland's games, helping the team to reach the semi-finals. He then moved to Old Trafford where he took his place at the heart of United's defence.

A favourite with the fans, Jaap was voted one of the club's top fifty players of all time half-way through his first season and for three months in a row was picked as United's player of the month.

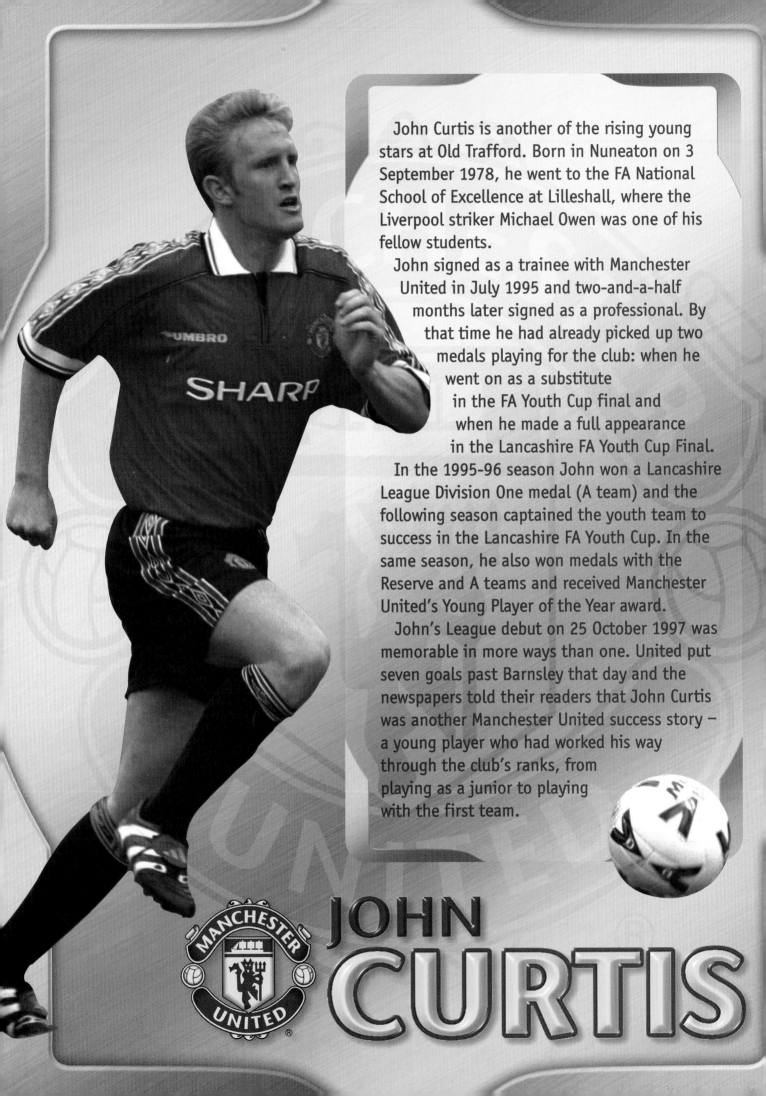

John Curtis is another of the rising young stars at Old Trafford. Born in Nuneaton on 3 September 1978, he went to the FA National School of Excellence at Lilleshall, where the Liverpool striker Michael Owen was one of his fellow students.

John signed as a trainee with Manchester United in July 1995 and two-and-a-half months later signed as a professional. By that time he had already picked up two medals playing for the club: when he went on as a substitute in the FA Youth Cup final and when he made a full appearance in the Lancashire FA Youth Cup Final. In the 1995-96 season John won a Lancashire League Division One medal (A team) and the following season captained the youth team to success in the Lancashire FA Youth Cup. In the same season, he also won medals with the Reserve and A teams and received Manchester United's Young Player of the Year award.

John's League debut on 25 October 1997 was memorable in more ways than one. United put seven goals past Barnsley that day and the newspapers told their readers that John Curtis was another Manchester United success story – a young player who had worked his way through the club's ranks, from playing as a junior to playing with the first team.

JOHN CURTIS

THE RED WEB

As you'd expect from the club at the leading edge of football, Manchester United has its own official web site on the internet - and you need just twelve letters to get in there:

WWW.MANUTD.COM

Log on to the club's web site and you'll find pages packed with up-to-the-minute information about players, fixtures and results, plus polls for fans to fill in, such as the latest 'Man of the Match', and special competitions, with prizes for the winners.

Browsing through, you'll find detailed information about topics like:

- NEWS
- MATCHES
- TEAM
- SUPPORTERS
- OLD TRAFFORD
- CONFERENCE & CATERING
- MEGASTORE
- MUTV
- SPONSORS

Elsewhere, you'll be able to click on to:

- LATEST NEWS
- FANS' QUESTIONS
- FIXTURES AND RESULTS
- MATCH REPORTS
- PREMIERSHIP TABLE
- UEFA CHAMPIONS LEAGUE
- TICKET INFORMATION
- TELEPHONE NUMBERS
- VIRTUAL REALITY TOUR
- INSIDE OLD TRAFFORD
- PLAYERS' BIOGRAPHIES
- DAVID MEEK

With all this to choose from you can make every day a 'home fixture' with United. But remember to get permission to log on from whoever pays the telephone bill.

IT'S A FACT

Though you may need no convincing, here are just some of the amazing facts and figures that help explain why Manchester United is the world's greatest football club.

Manchester United are the only club to have played in an FA Cup Final in every decade since the Second World War.

The scoreboard at Old Trafford once showed the highest ever score in a Premiership match. That was on 4 March 1995 when United beat Ipswich Town 9-0.

When Alex Ferguson signed as a player for Rangers in 1967, he set a record in Scottish football with a transfer fee of £55,000.

During the club's history two pairs of brothers have helped United win an FA Cup Final. In 1977 the brothers were Brian and Jimmy Greenhoff and in 1996 they were Phil and Gary Neville.

Alex Ferguson is the only manager to manage two European Cup Winners' Cup winning sides in different countries: Aberdeen in Scotland and Manchester United in England.

The North Stand at Old Trafford contains 4,000 tons of steel and 4,500 tons of concrete.

When they first started playing in European competitions United remained unbeaten at home for 40 years. The first goal scored against them came in a match played on 30 October 1996 against the Turkish side Fenerbahce SK, which the Turkish team won 1-0.

Manchester United is the only British club to have won both the European Cup and the European Cup Winners' Cup.

Whenever United play at home, fans coming to watch the game consume an incredible amount of food and drink. On average they eat 10,000 pies and drink 2,500 gallons of cola, tea and coffee.

David Beckham's famous long-distance goal, which he scored against Wimbledon on 17 August 1996, is the furthest successful shot on goal in the history of the Premiership.

The North Stand at Old Trafford can seat 25,110 spectators, which is more than can sit in the whole of the stadiums belonging to several clubs in the Premier League.

United's former captain, Steve Bruce, scored 11 penalties in the 1990-91 season – the highest total for a season by any United player.

During his time with the club, Eric Cantona took 19 penalties for Manchester United and scored all but two of them.

On Monday mornings as many as 800 pieces of Manchester United kit are washed in the club's special laundry at Old Trafford.

When Gary and Phil Neville played for England in the summer of 1996, they were the first brothers to play together in the England team since Bobby Charlton and Jack Charlton in the 1960s.

United didn't lose one of their home games in the Premiership during the 1995-96 season.

When United kicked off against Southampton on 18 November 1995, Ryan Giggs scored the fastest goal in the club's history, when he netted the ball in the first 16 seconds of the match! Four minutes later Giggs scored United's second and, with only eight minutes of the game gone, Paul Scholes put United 3-0 up. The game ended with United winning 4-0.

During the 1994-95 season David Beckham went on loan to Preston North End and scored goals playing for them in the Third Division. Back at Manchester United, in the same season, he was scoring in the UEFA Champions' League.

Mark Hughes won his first European Cup Winners' Cup medal playing for United in 1991 and won a second, seven years later, playing for Chelsea.

Sir Bobby Charlton holds three club records at Manchester United. He made the highest number of League appearances (606). He scored the highest number of League goals (199). And he is United's most capped player, having made 106 appearances for England.

Roy Keane played in four FA Cup Finals between 1991 and 1996. He played for Nottingham Forest in one and for Manchester United in the other three.

The record attendance at Old Trafford was set at an FA Cup semi-final in 1939, even though United were not playing. The two sides on the field that day were Wolves and Grimsby.

While he was playing for Ayr United, Alex Ferguson scored 10 goals in 24 matches.

United's former captain, Bryan Robson, is the only player in the 20th century to have captained three FA Cup-winning sides: in 1983, 1985 and 1990. He was the longest-serving captain in the history of the club, doing the job for 12 years, from 1982 to 1994.

When Ole Gunnar Solskjaer scored on his debut for Manchester United, he became the 87th player to do so.

Apart from his brilliant performances in the United goal, Peter Schmeichel also helped the club to an important home result on 26 September 1995. With only minutes of the game left, United were 2-1 down to the Russian side Rotor Volgograd. Then came a United corner and Schmeichel was brought up into the Russian penalty area. When the kick came in, he leapt into the air and scored his first ever goal for the club. The 2-2 draw meant that United kept their unbeaten home record in European competitions.

NO GROUNDS FOR COMPLAINT

All of the following clubs' grounds had their record attendances set by a visit from Manchester United.

Club	Ground	Year
AFC Bournemouth	Dean Court	1957
Hartlepool United	Victoria Park	1957
Hull City	Boothferry Park	1949
Nottingham Forest	City Ground	1967
Southampton	The Dell	1969
Watford	Vicarage Road	1969
Wimbledon	Selhurst Park	1993
Wrexham	The Racecourse	1957

Because everyone wants to see the Reds!

CROSSWORD CHALLENGE

Test your knowledge of your favourite team, and football generally, with this monster puzzle. The number in brackets shows the number of letters in each answer.

ACROSS

3   The start of the match (4-3)
5   Where fans used to stand at football matches (8)
8   (and 22 Down) Barcelona's home ground (4,3)
9   Solskjaer's middle name (6)
11 The best way of spending Saturday afternoon is to - - to the match (2)
12 Another name for a centre forward (7)
13 All the Red's players are this! (5)
14 A warming drink for half-time (3)
15 A shot above ground level (6)
17 Glenn Hoddle was England's - - - - - until early 1999 (5)
20 The nickname of West Ham United (7)
22 The name of Old Trafford's biggest rebuilt stand (5)
24 The name of Manchester United's manager (4, 8)
29 You might do this if you had to miss the match and do your homework instead! (5)
31 If your boot fits badly, you might get one of these on your foot (7)
35 The year 2000 (10)
36 What you feel when a United player scores a goal (6)
37 Another name for Tottenham Hotspur (5)
39 Without lights, you would be in this for an evening match (8)

DOWN

1   The name of the greatest game in the world (6)
2   Henning's surname (4)
3   Sir Matt Busby's title made him one of these (6)
4   A trophy (3)
6   What you sit on, or the head of a company (5)
7   If you're this, you can run round the field quickly (6)
10 Alex, the player's, surname (6)
12 Schmeichel might make a great one (4)
16 Formed in 1888 the Football - - - - - - has four divisions (6)
17 A free kick might be this (6)
18 Each half of the match takes three-quarters of this (4)
19 If a ball hits you hard on the shin you might say this! (4)
21 What I call myself (2)
22 See 8 Across
23 You, your dog and each of your boots has one! (6)
25 Manchester's county (10)
26 The Football Association (1, 1)
27 He might save the day! (10)
28 Winter is traditionally the football - - - - - - (6)
30 Where the F.A. Cup Final takes place (7)
32 Another word for stories you might hear, e.g. about a transfer (7)
33 Johan is this to Jordi (6)
34 Solskjaer's first name (3)
38 What you do after the ball (3)

JESPER BLOMQVIST

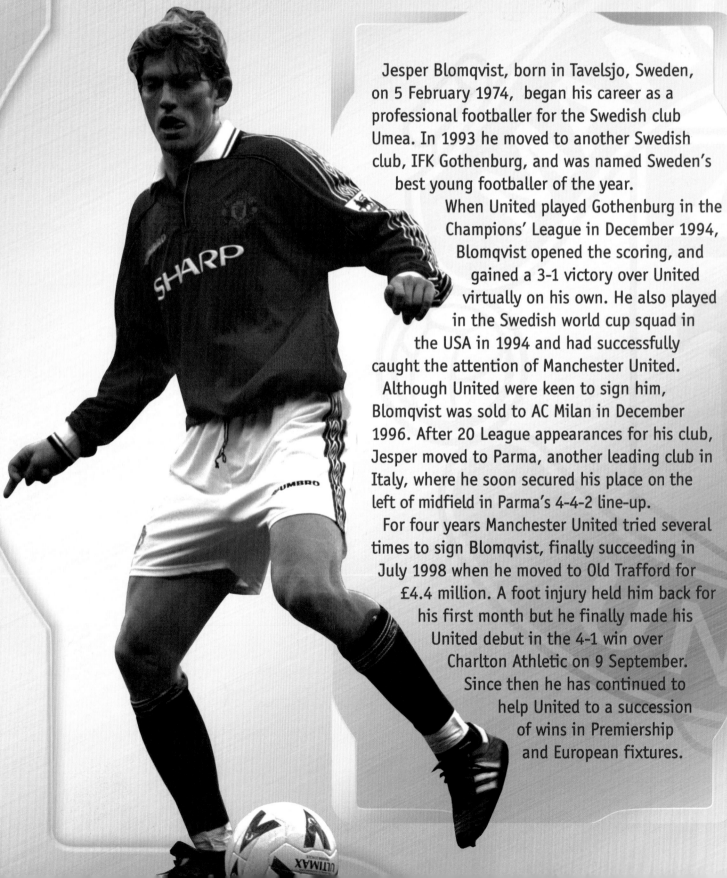

Jesper Blomqvist, born in Tavelsjo, Sweden, on 5 February 1974, began his career as a professional footballer for the Swedish club Umea. In 1993 he moved to another Swedish club, IFK Gothenburg, and was named Sweden's best young footballer of the year.

When United played Gothenburg in the Champions' League in December 1994, Blomqvist opened the scoring, and gained a 3-1 victory over United virtually on his own. He also played in the Swedish world cup squad in the USA in 1994 and had successfully caught the attention of Manchester United.

Although United were keen to sign him, Blomqvist was sold to AC Milan in December 1996. After 20 League appearances for his club, Jesper moved to Parma, another leading club in Italy, where he soon secured his place on the left of midfield in Parma's 4-4-2 line-up.

For four years Manchester United tried several times to sign Blomqvist, finally succeeding in July 1998 when he moved to Old Trafford for £4.4 million. A foot injury held him back for his first month but he finally made his United debut in the 4-1 win over Charlton Athletic on 9 September. Since then he has continued to help United to a succession of wins in Premiership and European fixtures.

Manchester born and bred, Wesley Brown was spotted by the former United player Harry McShane when he was playing in an Under-12s match. In July 1996 he signed with United as a trainee and four months later joined the club as a professional.

Wesley attended the FA School of Excellence at Lilleshall, where Michael Owen was one of his classmates. In the 1996-1997 season, he collected a Lancashire FA Youth Cup winners medal and a Lancashire Division One championship medal. In the following season, he picked up a Lancashire League Division One medal and won the Denzil Haroun Young Player of the Year Award. This run of success earned him a first-team debut when United played Leeds at Old Trafford on 4 May 1998.

In the 1998-1999 season, Wesley played regularly in the first team, covering the full back position when Denis Irwin was injured. On top of his club success, Wesley has played for England at Under 18s and Under 21s level and has been invited to travel with the full international squad.

WESLEY BROWN

Yesterday you scored a STUNNING hat-trick against the strongest defence in Europe, but now you have to report for training.

'Make-It-Up' Maurice
ace news-hound

'Red-Eye' Reagan
demon photographer

Can you find a way to the training ground, avoiding the WORST of the World's Press?

START HERE

Viddy O'Footidge
gritty cameraman

Mike Raffowen
fiery radio reporter

TRAINING GROUND

BIRTHDAY NEWS

What was going on at Manchester United in the year you were born? From the season in which Alex Ferguson became United's manager to the season in which the club won its first ever double, here are some of the key dates and headline events in the life of the club and its players.

 1986–87

17 November 1986 – Alex Ferguson was appointed Manager of Manchester United
United's youth team ended the season Lancashire League Division One ("A" team) champions

 1987–88

1 July 1987 – Brian McClair signed for United
17 December 1987 – Steve Bruce signed for United
April 1988 – Brian McClair scored his 20th League goal of the season. This made him the first United player to do so since George Best, 20 years earlier
United ended the season as First Division runners-up
United's youth team ended the season Lancashire League Division One ("A" team) champions

 1988–89

1 June 1988 – Lee Sharpe signed for United
July 1988 – Mark Hughes signed for United
April 1989 – Mark Hughes was awarded PFA Player of the Year
United's youth team ended the season Lancashire League Division Two ("B" team) champions

 1989–90

28 August 1989 – Gary Pallister signed for United
September 1989 – Paul Ince and Danny Wallace signed for United
United won the FA Cup and Bryan Robson became the first-ever player to captain a team to three FA Cup wins
United's youth team ended the season Lancashire League Division One ("A" team) champions

 1990–91

8 June 1990 – Denis Irwin signed for United
9 July 1990 – Ryan Giggs signed for United as a trainee
29 November 1990 – Ryan Giggs signed for United as a professional
March 1991 – Mark Hughes was awarded PFA Player of the Year for a second time
United's youth team ended the season Lancashire League Division One ("A" team) champions
The United youth team also won the Lancashire FA Youth Cup

 1991–92

Jim Ryan was appointed Reserve Team Coach
8 July 1991 – David Beckham, Gary Neville and Paul Scholes signed for United as trainees

6 August 1991 – Peter Schmeichel and Paul Parker signed for United

April 1992 – Ryan Giggs was awarded PFA Young Player of the Year and Gary Pallister was voted Player of the Year

United ended the season as winners of the League Cup and the European Super Cup, and runners-up in the First Division

The United Youth team, which included David Beckham, Nicky Butt and Gary Neville, won the FA Youth Cup

 1992–93

1 July 1992 – Raimond Van Der Gouw signed for United

August 1992 – Steve Bruce was appointed team captain

27 November 1992 – Eric Cantona signed for United

23 January 1993 – David Beckham, Nicky Butt, Gary Neville and Paul Scholes signed for United as professionals

February 1993 – Peter Schmeichel was made Premier League Goalkeeper of the Year

April 1993 – Ryan Giggs was awarded PFA Young Player of the Year for the second time, the first player ever to receive the title twice

United ended the season Premier League champions

United's youth team ended the season Lancashire League Division One ("A" team) champions

The United youth team also won the Lancashire FA Youth Cup

 1993–94

5 July 1993 – Phil Neville and Michael Clegg signed for United as trainees

19 July 1993 – Roy Keane signed for United

20 January 1994 – Sir Matt Busby, United's famous manager who brought the European

Cup back to Old Trafford in 1968, died

March 1994 – Eric Cantona was awarded PFA Player of the Year, the first foreign player to receive the title

United ended the season Premier League champions, FA Cup winners and League Cup finalists – the club had won the double for the first time in its history

The United youth team also won the Lancashire FA Youth Cup

 # BIRTHDAY BOYS

Do you share the same birthday as any of United's stars?

UNITED PLAYER	BIRTHDAY
Peter Schmeichel	18 November
Gary Neville	18 February
Denis Irwin	31 October
David May	24 June
Ronny Johnsen	10 June
Jaap Stam	17 July
David Beckham	02 May
Nicky Butt	21 January
Andrew Cole	15 October
Teddy Sheringham	02 April
Ryan Giggs	29 November
Phil Neville	21 January
Jordi Cruyff	09 February
Roy Keane	10 August
Raimond Van Der Gouw	24 March
Paul Scholes	16 November
Dwight Yorke	03 November
Ole Gunnar Solskjaer	26 February
Henning Berg	01 September
Jesper Blomqvist	05 February
Wes Brown	16 March
John Curtis	03 September
And the manager . . ?	
Alex Ferguson	31 December

UNITED AWAY

Gary Neville
Man Utd v Charlton

Roy Keane, David Beckham and Paul Scholes
Man Utd v Barcelona

Roy Keane
Man Utd v Arsenal

Ole Gunnar Solskjaer
Man Utd v Arsenal

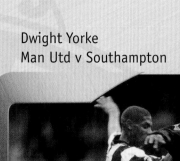

Dwight Yorke
Man Utd v Southampton

David Beckham
Man Utd v Arsenal

Dwight Yorke
Man Utd v Barcelona

Ryan Giggs
Man Utd v Charlton

TRAINING FOR THE NEXT CENTURY

It's nearly fifty years since Manchester United moved into the Cliff, the club's main training ground in Salford, not far from Old Trafford. During that time, United's stars have trained and practised both there and at nearby Littleton Road, where the club has another large training area.

The manager and players spend most of their working time at these two places. The players train for two hours each morning on a non-match day, some of them staying on for extra training to get them into peak condition.

As well as one full-sized football pitch and one smaller one, the Cliff has a full-sized indoor pitch with an Astroturf surface, a gym, changing rooms, a canteen and rooms to study tactics. The club physiotherapist is also based at the Cliff, where his room is kitted out with special equipment to treat injuries and help the players back to full fitness.

The training grounds may have seen many great moments in the club's history, but as Manchester United looks towards the next century, it's clear that it needs a larger, more up-to-date training base. Hence, in the spring of 1998, the club announced their plans to develop a state of the art training centre seven miles from Old Trafford, at Carrington in south-west Manchester. When this opens in 2000, the 100-acre site will have nine full-sized grass pitches, four junior pitches and several specialised training areas,

including one for goalkeepers. These training areas are for the United stars of the future and the Manchester United Academy will be based there.

For several years, Manchester United has been running a School of Excellence, coaching promising young players. In the summer of 1998, it was renamed the Manchester United Academy and new FA rules enabled them to coach boys from under-nine right through to 21. The Academy offers the young players quality coaching, comfortable training areas to develop their skills, and medical and physiotherapy aid. As they grow older they are advised by a welfare service which helps them to plan for the future. The Academy also ensures that the young players receive a good education alongside their football training and that they are given chores in order to teach them self-discipline and responsibility. When their time as trainees comes to an end, the manager decides whether to sign them as professional players.

Not all trainees become professionals and Manchester United advises those who don't and helps them to find new clubs.

Although United will be moving training grounds very shortly, it will be sticking by one of its most important traditions - finding young players and coaching them up through the club's youth teams to its senior sides. And with the club's junior sides, the reserves and the first-team all training there, the new training centre is going to be a centre of footballing excellence like no other.

Only one of the mirrored pictures is exactly the same as this. Which one?

31

MINI QUIZ

ALL AT 'C'

We hope you're not all at sea with these United posers.
All the answers begin with the letter 'C'.

1   Which of United's Premiership rivals play at home at Stamford Bridge?

2   Which United star holds the record for goals scored in a Premiership season?

3   Which United player joined the club from Barcelona?

4   'C' if you know which United legend won a World Cup Winners' medal?

5   Ryan Giggs was born in which city?

6   Phil Neville made his England debut against which country?

7   Who scored United's winner in the 1996 FA Cup Final?

8   Denis Irwin and Roy Keane are both from . . . ?

9   Phil Neville was asked to play which sport for England at Junior level?

10   And finally – Manchester United have been Top of the Premiership more
     times than anyone else?

TAKEN AS RED

We've set a few posers for you. All you need to do is
fill in the blanks, but include the letters RED consecutively.

1   Dwight Yorke, the ultimate p----tor.

2   Everyone's favourite mascot is ----.

3   Brian Kidd was Steve McLaren's p------essor.

4   Unbelievable, inc-----le! That's a Beckham free kick.

5   Harry ~~Redkna~~-p, manager of United's Premiership rivals West Ham.

6   Dwight and Andrew can tear a defence to -h----.

32

BECK TO SKOOL

David Beckham is famous for keeping opposing players guessing – now see if you can work out the answers to these sums using his and other United players' 1998-99 squad numbers.

1	Denis Irwin + Jaap Stam	= ?
2	? + Dwight Yorke	= Wes Brown
3	Phil Neville + ?	= Dwight Yorke
4	? - Roy Keane	= David May
5	David Beckham x Denis Irwin	= ?
6	Ronny Johnsen + ?	= Phil Neville
7	Ryan Giggs – David Beckham	= ?
8	Henning Berg ÷ Denis Irwin	= ?
9	Nicky Butt x Gary Neville	= ?
10	? ÷ ?	= Jesper Blomqvist

ANYONE FOR SECONDS?

1   United's first Double was clinched in 1994. What year saw their second Double?

2   United's first European trophy was the European Cup. What was their second trophy?

3   Paul Scholes was the first United star to score in the 1998 World Cup. Who was the second?

4   United were the first team to do the double Double. Who were the second?

5   United were the first team to win the Premiership. Who were the second?

6   Ryan Giggs's first name is Ryan. What is his second (and don't answer "Giggs").

7   Listed in alphabetical order, David Beckham is currently the first United first-team player. Who is the second?

8   United first won the Premiership in 1993. When were they Premiership champions for the second time?

9   Bobby Charlton was the first player to score over 48 goals for England. Who was the second?

10   Denis Irwin's first club was Leeds United. What was his second?

THE WORLD OF MANCHESTER UNITED

You'd expect the world's greatest football club to have a worldwide following and with Manchester United you won't be disappointed. From Tokyo, the capital of Japan, to Toronto, the largest city in Canada, there are official Manchester United overseas supporters' clubs right round the world. And as you can see from the pictures, many of them are in places a lot warmer and drier than Old Trafford!

Our world tour kicks off closest to home, in Europe. That's where you'll find most of United's supporters' clubs. As you'd expect, the greatest number of these are in the UK and Ireland. But United are well-represented in the rest of Europe, too – as you can see . . .

BELGIUM

United contact:
Peter Bauwens
Merellaan 52
9060 Zelzate
Belgium
Tel: 00 32 934 40578

Phil Mulryne, United's young Northern Ireland midfielder, scored his first international goal when he went on as a substitute against Belgium in February 1997. But Belgian Reds don't hold that against their favourite club.

CYPRUS

United contact:
Ronis Soteriades
PO Box 1365
3504 Limassol
Cyprus
Tel: 00 357 5 337690
Fax: 00 357 5 388652

Cyprus is an island in the eastern Mediterranean. It's one of those places which has brilliant weather all year round, even in winter. In Cyprus it's possible to go skiing in the mountains in the morning and go swimming in the sea after lunch – not bad, eh? No wonder it's such a popular holiday island. No wonder, too, that several British football clubs pick Cyprus for warm-weather training.

DENMARK

United contact:
Helge Conradsen
Varminglundvej 13
DK-6760 Ribe
Denmark
Tel: 00 45 7544 1396

No prizes for guessing United's connection with Denmark – if you need a clue, try the letters PS. Yes, Peter Schmeichel comes from Denmark and in his last season with United the Great Dane helped his Old Trafford team mates defeat his former club, Danish champions Brondby, in the Champions' League. In the away leg United won 6-2 and, back at Old Trafford they put five past the Danish side – better still, big Peter kept a clean sheet that night.

GERMANY

United contact:
Ulrich Heumann
German Reds
Frankensteiner Strasse 3
D59269 Beckum
Germany
Tel: 00 49 2521 16353

Germany is the home of some mighty football clubs, several of which United has come up against in the Champions' League in recent years. It also has a good many red-hot United supporters. There are three official supporters' clubs, of which the oldest and largest is German Reds.

GIBRALTAR

United contact:
Gerald Laguea
Manchester United
Supporters Gibraltar
Branch
PO Box 22
Gibraltar
Tel/Fax: 00 350 50822

Gibraltar may be closer to the Sahara Desert than it is to Old . Trafford, but there's no doubting the loyalty of the United supporters who follow their team, week in week out. In 1962, Sir Matt Busby, who was the Manchester United Manager at the time, gave his permission for a local football club in Gibraltar to use the name Manchester United and the club colours. They've been doing this ever since and, like their namesakes at Old Trafford, they've been champions on numerous occasions.

ICELAND

United contact:
Bubbi Avesson
Studningsmannaklubbur
Manchester United a
Isländî
PO Box 12170
132 Reykjavik
Iceland

The name Iceland may sound a bit on the chilly side, but this island actually has a higher average temperature through the year than New York City, which is hundreds of miles further south, on the east coast of the USA! Maybe it's supporting the Reds that keeps them warm.

LUXEMBOURG

United contact:
Steve Kaiser
2 Vir Resichtert
L-6948 Niederanven
Luxembourg
Tel: 00 352 340265

Luxembourg may be one of the smallest countries in Europe, but it still has plenty of Manchester United supporters. They follow their team's performances on the pitch at home in England and when they travel to Europe itself, to take on the competition in the Champions' League.

MALTA

United contact:
Randolph Mizzi
MUSC Malta
Quarries Square
Msida
MSD 03
Malta
Tel: 00 356 223531
Fax: 00 356 231902

There are about 20,000 Manchester United supporters on the island of Malta. The Manchester United Supporters' Club (Malta) is well supported by them and by the island's youngsters – there are nearly 200 under-12 members! Whenever United are playing, members gather to watch United's games on the giant screen at the supporters' club and when the reds score, you'd think you could hear the cheering in Msida back in Manchester!

NETHERLANDS

United contact:
Ron Snellen
PO Box 33742
2503 BA Den Haag
Netherlands
Tel: 00 31 70 329 8602
Fax: 00 31 70 367 2247

With Dutch players Jaap Stam, the world's most expensive defender, Raimond van der Gouw and Jordi Cruyff playing for Manchester United, it's little wonder that United have a supporters' club in the Netherlands. Dutch football has some impressive teams, so it's a credit to United that it can attract a loyal following in the Netherlands, even in the face of stiff local competition.

NORWAY

Norway is the home of Ronny Johnsen, Henning Berg, Ole Gunnar Solskjaer and Erik Nevland – but United had a loyal following in Norway even before this fearsome foursome arrived at Old Trafford. Today, the support for them and the rest of the United team is stronger than ever in Norway.

United contact:
Per H. Larsen
PO Box 4003 Dreggen
N-5023 Bergen
Norway
Tel: 00 47 5531 3889
Fax: 00 47 5596 2033

SWEDEN

Swedish Reds have had something extra special to cheer about since United acquired the speedy services of ace Swedish winger Jesper Blomqvist. Jesper started his playing career in Sweden, though when United bought him he was playing with top-flight teams in Italy.

United contact:
Kent Yxell
Västra
Långattan 4a
S-374 33 Karlshamn
Sweden
Tel: 00 46 454 31 763
(after 14.00)

SWITZERLAND

Switzerland has German football clubs to the north, Italian clubs to the south and French ones to the west – and the likes of Rapid Vienna over the eastern border in Austria. These teams have all given United a run for their money in European competitions. Surrounded by some of the best football in Europe and producing impressive teams of their own, there are still a good number of Swiss Devils keen to show their loyalty to Manchester United.

United contact:
Mark Tanner
Soodstrasse 64
8134 Adliswil
Switzerland
Tel: 00 41 1 710 5986/ 00
41 1 267 5513
Fax: 00 41 1 252 20 02

THE WORLD OF MANCHESTER UNITED

Of course, the real mark of a world-class club is world-class support. Take a look at United's official supporters' clubs spread right round the world. And then think about the thousands and thousands of other supporters, many of them in other countries, who proudly wear United kit and can reel off the names of Alex Ferguson's squad quicker than they can name the politicians who run their own governments. Is it any wonder United attract massive crowds wherever they travel, no matter how far they are from Old Trafford?

AUSTRALIA

A huge country like Australia needs more than one United supporters' club – in fact there are four!

United contacts:
NEW SOUTH WALES
Graham Shakespeare
PO Box 693
Sutherland 2232
New South Wales
Australia
Tel/Fax: 00 61 2 9589 2578

SOUTH AUSTRALIA
PO Box 276
Ingle Farm
South Australia 5098
Fax: 00 61 8 82816731

VICTORIA
Kieran Dunleavy
PO Box 1199
Camberwell
3124 Victoria
Australia
Tel/Fax: 00 62 39 804 0244

WESTERN AUSTRALIA
Graham Wyche
19 Frobisher Avenue
Sorrento 6020
Perth
Western Australia
Tel/Fax: 00 61 89 447 1144

CANADA

Canada is the second largest country in the world and has the longest coastline. Manchester United has supporters right across Canada, from the Atlantic Ocean to the Pacific Ocean.

United contact:
Manchester United
Supporters Club
12 St Clair Avenue East
PO Box 69057
Toronto
Ontario
M4T 3AI
Canada

HONG KONG

Manchester United are well supported in Hong Kong. The official supporters' club has well over 1,200 members. Added to them are several thousand other loyal followers. The Manchester United Supporters' Club (Hong Kong) produces a newsletter called 'Simply Reds'. Drop a line to the club if you want to make a United pen-pal in Hong Kong.

United contact:
Paul J. Kam
Manchester United
Supporters Club (Hong Kong)
Suite 816
New Commerce Centre
19 On Sum Street
Siu Lek Yeun
Shatin
Hong Kong
Fax: 00 852 2314 7282

JAPAN

Football is growing fast in Japan, as it is in many other countries around the Pacific Ocean. Manchester United have strong contacts with Japan and the club is well-supported by British people living in Japan, as well as Japanese fans.

United contact (English information):
Steve Ryan
Tel: 00 81 3 3380 8441

MALAYSIA

Malaysia is a very friendly place. United players know this from their tours to the Far East and United supporters are always made welcome by the official supporters' club. They have two 'outposts' where visiting supporters can drop in to have a chat and meet fellow Reds.

United contact:
Laurence How
47a Jalan SS 2/75
47300 Petaling Jaya
Selangor
D.E. Malaysia
Tel: 00 60 3 7773070
& 00 60 3 7775339
Fax: 00 60 3 7774511

MAURITIUS

Mauritius is a beautiful, tropical country, and the perfect place for a holiday. Pity it's so far away. Still, Mauritius isn't too far away to watch United on television. There's a cable service that brings the games to these supporters, right out in the Indian Ocean. Sun, sand, sea and United beamed in on televsion – it can't be bad, can it?

United contact:
Atchia Yacoob
Flamingo Pool House
Remeno Street
Rose Hill
Thantitius
Mauritius
Fax: 00 230 4543570

NEW ZEALAND

The Manchester United supporters' club in New Zealand is the furthest official branch club from Old Trafford. Because the time in New Zealand is twelve hours ahead of time in the UK, the time there is three o'clock on Sunday morning when it's kick-off at three o'clock on Saturday afternoon at Old Trafford.

United contact:
Brian Wood
3 Drummond Street
Whangerai
New Zealand
Tel: 00 64 9
4396140/4385650

SOUTH AFRICA

In South Africa, United supporters are able to watch their team live on television, thanks to SATV. Football is developing fast in South Africa, which means that support there for the world's greatest football club can only grow and grow. It's a happy coincidence, then, that South Africa played an international fixture against England at Old Trafford in May 1997.

United contact:
Ethel Sleith
PO Box 13990
Witfield 1467
South Africa
Tel/Fax: 00 27 826 2181

USA

The official Manchester United spporters' club in the USA is on the north-east coast, but support for the club spreads right across America. Thousands of American supporters tune in to watch all United's games and soccer (that's to distinguish the game from American football) is probably the biggest recreational sport in many areas of the USA, especially among kids.

United contact:
Peter Holland
MUSC USA HQ
139 West Neck Road
Huntingdon
N.Y. 11743
USA
Tel: 00 1 516 547 5500
Fax: 00 1 516 547 6800

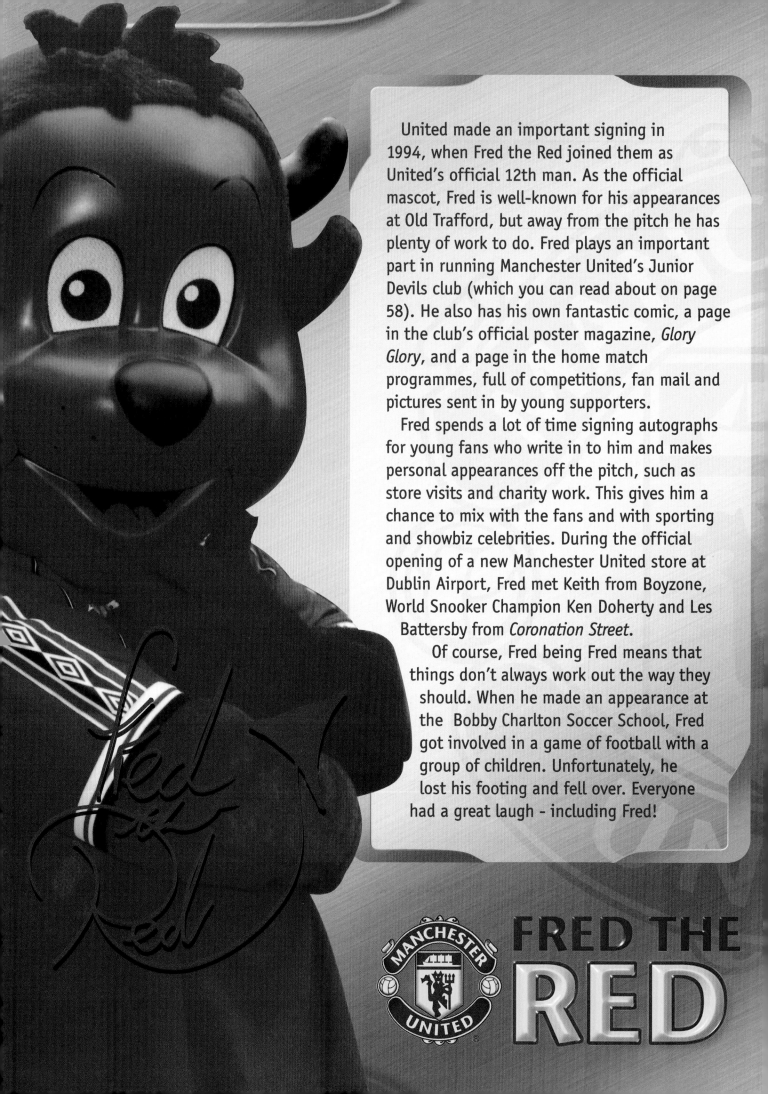

United made an important signing in 1994, when Fred the Red joined them as United's official 12th man. As the official mascot, Fred is well-known for his appearances at Old Trafford, but away from the pitch he has plenty of work to do. Fred plays an important part in running Manchester United's Junior Devils club (which you can read about on page 58). He also has his own fantastic comic, a page in the club's official poster magazine, *Glory Glory*, and a page in the home match programmes, full of competitions, fan mail and pictures sent in by young supporters.

Fred spends a lot of time signing autographs for young fans who write in to him and makes personal appearances off the pitch, such as store visits and charity work. This gives him a chance to mix with the fans and with sporting and showbiz celebrities. During the official opening of a new Manchester United store at Dublin Airport, Fred met Keith from Boyzone, World Snooker Champion Ken Doherty and Les Battersby from *Coronation Street*.

Of course, Fred being Fred means that things don't always work out the way they should. When he made an appearance at the Bobby Charlton Soccer School, Fred got involved in a game of football with a group of children. Unfortunately, he lost his footing and fell over. Everyone had a great laugh - including Fred!

FRED THE RED

A Day In The Life Of
FRED THE RED

Match day for Fred is full of excitement, especially when United are playing at home. Like the rest of the team, Fred follows a set timetable, which begins from the time he arrives at the stadium.

This is his own special programme.

FRED'S PROGRAMME

12.00 – Fred arrives at the stadium, where he has his pre-match meal, like the other players.

2.00 – Fred changes into his strip.

2.30 – Fred greets the mascots who will be going out with the team at the start of the match. He signs autographs and has his picture taken with them. Then it's time to get down to work, out in the stadium itself.

2.45 – Fred entertains fans inside the stadium. He goes round the pitch, doing various popular warm-up routines and other exercises to delight the fans. He also signs autographs and poses for pictures. When there are players warming up, Fred has a joke around with them – two of his particular pals are David May and Raimond Van Der Gouw.

2.55 – Fred goes to the entrance of the players' tunnel, where he awaits the teams when they run out on to the pitch.

3.00 – Fred greets the players as they run on to the pitch. Then he waits at the dug-outs for the mascots, who run back to him after they have walked out with the teams. He then escorts them back to the dressing-rooms.

3.45 – Half-time. While the players are back in the dressing-rooms, Fred is in action again inside the stadium, doing his lap of honour, entertaining the fans and providing more autographs and photographs.

4.00 – After the game, Fred goes back to the dressing-rooms to have a shower and change out of his kit.

4.45 – Fred leaves the stadium and returns home. The following morning it's back to work when the postman brings his next delivery of fan mail. And then there's the next home game to look forward to and the prospect of another brilliant game for Fred and the rest of the Reds.

CELEBRATION!

THE ODD SQUAD

There are eleven players who have exact doubles on this training ground. Can you find them all?

YOUNG GUNS

As juniors they were known as Fergie's Fledglings. When five of them were picked to play for their country (England) they became Young Lions – presumably that made the sixth a Young Dragon when he won his Welsh cap. Now they're all well-established first-team players with their names on the FA and Premiership trophies at home, plus a growing string of successes in Europe under their belts. They are (in case you didn't know) Manchester United's Young Guns: David Beckham, Nicky Butt, Ryan Giggs, Gary Neville, Phil Neville and Paul Scholes.

It was as Fergie's Fledglings that they began to attract attention outside United's training grounds – and this was no coincidence. All through his time as a football manager, Alex Ferguson has believed in the importance of building strong youth sides, where young players can get the best coaching, the best training and the best advice right at the start of their football careers. This system helps youngsters develop inside the club and gives them the chance to play their way up, through the junior sides to the senior teams, it has paid off at all Alex Ferguson's clubs. It's at Manchester United where it has probably had its greatest success.

Alex Ferguson took over as United's Manager in November 1986. At that time, many of the best young players in the Manchester area were being signed up for other clubs – and United were losing out. The new manager put a stop to this and word went out to every youth team in the area (as well as the rest of the country) that Manchester United was now the club to join.

By 1992 the standard of United's youth teams was no longer in doubt. Alex Ferguson felt confident that his youngsters would end the season as champions, and they didn't let him down – in the final they beat Crystal Palace and lifted the FA Youth Cup. Among the players in that championship side were: David Beckham, Nicky Butt, Ryan Giggs and Gary Neville. Paul Scholes and Phil Neville soon joined their team mates in the honours table. Along with the rest of that talented crop of youngsters, they gave Manchester United a strong group of home-grown players with all the determination, eagerness and skill needed to take on the best teams, at home and in Europe, in the years ahead.

DAVID BECKHAM

David Beckham made his mark at Old Trafford when he was just eleven years old, winning a Bobby Charlton Soccer Skills competition there. In 1991 he returned to sign as a trainee and by 1992 was part of the successful FA Youth Cup team which won the championship.

By 1993, Beckham had made his debut in the first team, playing in the last 20 minutes of a League Cup second round tie, and in his European debut in December 1994, he scored in front of his home crowd. His League debut came just six months later, and a spell on loan to Preston North End brought him several Man of the Match awards.

By the double-winning season of 1995-96, David was a permanent member of the United first-team and one of the most talked about players in the Premiership. In the following season, he played for England for the first time, having already won caps at youth and under-21 level. At the end of the season, he was voted PFA Young Player of the Year and he came second in the PFA Player of the Year poll.

Today, David Beckham is respected by his fellow footballers and by millions of adoring fans around the globe. Long may his success continue!

NICKY BUTT

Nicky Butt became a professional with the club in January 1993 and when Paul Ince left United in the summer of 1995, Nicky moved into midfield position, alongside Roy Keane. There, his tough-tackling, quick-thinking and sure-fire passing opened up dozens of counter-attacks. Coupled with his ability to make powerful attacking runs himself, Nicky has proved to be a very valuable player for United, and a great threat to the opposition.

On top of his success with Manchester United, Nicky Butt has represented England from schoolboy to full international level. Glen Hoddle regularly included him in his England squad and Hoddle's successor, Kevin Keegan, also recognised the young Butt as a future England star, saying, "Nicky's a tough little character. I think he's got a tremendous future at international level".

RYAN GIGGS

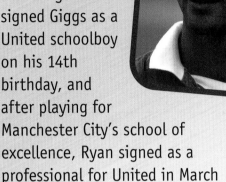

Alex Ferguson signed Giggs as a United schoolboy on his 14th birthday, and after playing for Manchester City's school of excellence, Ryan signed as a professional for United in March 1991, aged 17.

In his first-team debut, he went on as a substitute for Denis Irwin, and when Lee Sharpe was injured at the start of the 1991-2 season, Giggs took over on United's left wing, spearheading season after season of breathtaking United attacks that brought the club every senior footballing trophy in England.

As an international, Giggs was the youngest ever to play for Wales, at 17 years and 321 days old. He also captained the England Schoolboys team, having gone to school in England, though he is a true Welshman on and off the pitch.

Today, Giggs is one of the most respected and feared players in European football. His brilliant goal in United's 3-2 defeat of Juventus, in October 1997, is one example of his dazzling skill. He has twice been voted PFA Young Player of the Year and at the end of 1998, United fans voted him third in a list of the club's 50 greatest players of all time.

PHIL NEVILLE

As the youngest United player to win the double, Phil Neville got used to success with Manchester United early in his club career. Before joining United he had played for Bury Schools and Greater Manchester Schoolboys. He signed as a trainee with the club in July 1993 and became a professional less than a year later.

In 1995 he made his League debut in a Manchester Derby, when United travelled to Maine Road to play Manchester City. In the same year, Phil captained United's youth team to victory in the 1995 FA Youth Cup.

His success at club level caught the attention of England managers Terry Venables and Glenn Hoddle, who both included him in their England squads. In 1996 Gary and Phil Neville played for England, making them the first brothers to play together in the England team since United's great player, Sir Bobby Charlton, played in the England team with his brother Jack in the 1960s.

February 1998 brought another high point for Phil Neville when he coolly slotted home his first first-team goal against Chelsea at Stamford Bridge.

GARY NEVILLE

In March 1998, Gary Neville wore the Manchester United captain's armband for the first time and called it 'The greatest personal honour I've ever had ... or ever could have.' For a player who has supported United since he first went to watch his team when he was four years old, you can see what he means.

When he was 10, Gary went for trials with United and joined the club's school of excellence. As a teenager he played for Boundary Park Juniors alongside his brother, Phil, and their future United team mates: Nicky Butt and Paul Scholes. No wonder that team went undefeated for four seasons.

Gary signed for United as a trainee in July 1991 and became a professional with the club in January 1993. He played in United's successful Youth sides in 1992 and 1993. His League debut followed in May 1994 and when Paul Parker was injured in the 1994-95 season, Gary took over from him at full back. Since then, he has become a key player in United's defence, where his skill and success has led to an England call-up and a regular place in the England team.

PAUL SCHOLES

Paul Scholes was born in Salford, close to Old Trafford. He joined Manchester United as a trainee in July 1991 and by the time he signed as a professional, in January 1993, he had already picked up an FA Youth Cup winners' medal.

Paul made his League debut for United in September 1994, scoring twice against Ipswich Town. When United had to do without Eric Cantona and Mark Hughes later in the season, Paul became a regular first-team player. The following season, he was a member of United's historic double Double winning side, when the club won the Premier League title and the F.A. Cup in the same season for the second time.

Paul Scholes's powerful shots soon made him a regular member of the England team. In European matches he proved better than many top defenders, firing home memorable strikes against Juventus in 1997 and Inter Milan in 1999, to name just two of his famously important goals for United.

A
B
C
D
E
F

The boots on the left are paired with the boots on the right, but the laces that join them have got into a tangle. Can you work out which boot belongs to which?

IT'S **KNOT** easy!

1

2

3

4

5

6

COLOUR IN OUTLINES

YOU'RE THE REF

How well do you know the football rule book?
Well enough to be the referee in a United first-team game?
Take a look at these imaginary situations and see if you
know the correct decision the referee should take.

A penalty kick is taken by Denis
Irwin which rebounds from the post
without being touched by the
goalkeeper. Denis then slots in the
rebound, past the helpless keeper -
what do you award?

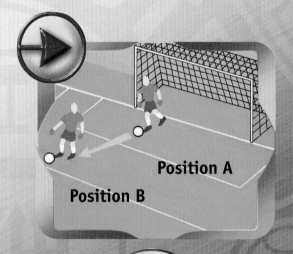

Position A

Position B

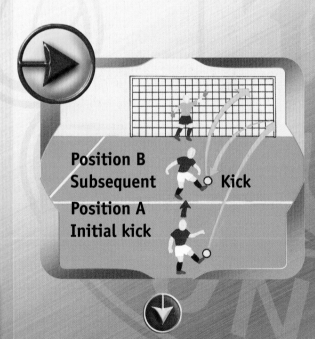

Position B
Subsequent ○ **Kick**

Position A
Initial kick

The United keeper takes a goal kick
but unfortunately mis-kicks so that
the ball does not leave the penalty
area. The keeper then kicks the ball
again - what should you award.

Answer
A goal kick - a penalty can not be
kicked twice by the same player
unless played by another player of
either side in between.

Answer
An indirect free kick to the
opposition.

54

A long throw-in is taken by Gary Neville but the ball eludes everyone and goes straight into the net - what is your decision.

A David Beckham special free kick is slightly off target for once and accidently strikes the Referee. The ball is deflected by the Referee, into the goal - what should you award.

Answer
A goal. The Referee is simply part of the field of play, like any other player - so however unfortunate, or fortunate, a goal results.

Answer
Give a goal kick. A goal cannot be scored direct from a throw-in.

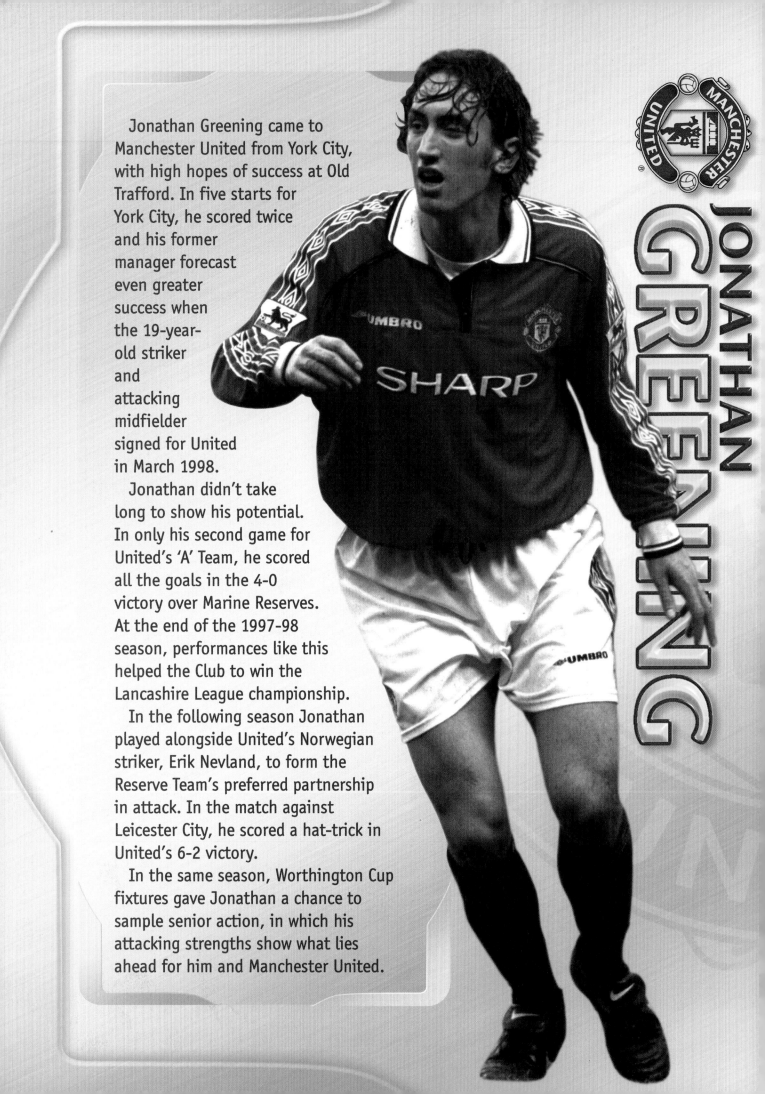

Jonathan Greening came to Manchester United from York City, with high hopes of success at Old Trafford. In five starts for York City, he scored twice and his former manager forecast even greater success when the 19-year-old striker and attacking midfielder signed for United in March 1998.

Jonathan didn't take long to show his potential. In only his second game for United's 'A' Team, he scored all the goals in the 4-0 victory over Marine Reserves. At the end of the 1997-98 season, performances like this helped the Club to win the Lancashire League championship.

In the following season Jonathan played alongside United's Norwegian striker, Erik Nevland, to form the Reserve Team's preferred partnership in attack. In the match against Leicester City, he scored a hat-trick in United's 6-2 victory.

In the same season, Worthington Cup fixtures gave Jonathan a chance to sample senior action, in which his attacking strengths show what lies ahead for him and Manchester United.

JONATHAN GREENING

Phil Mulryne is one of the talented young players who are sharpening their skills as they work their way up the United ladder.

Phil joined United as a trainee in the summer of 1994 and the following March signed for the club as a professional player. In 1995 he played in the Manchester United FA Youth Cup-winning side and, in the following year he picked up a Lancashire FA Youth Cup winners' medal.

On top of his success with Manchester United, Phil Mulryne is already an experienced player on the international scene. He made his debut for Northern Ireland in February 1997, when he went on as a substitute in the game against Belgium and scored – not a bad way to start.

His debut with the United first team came the following season, when Phil was picked to play against Ipswich Town in the Coca-Cola Cup, and he made his Premiership debut right at the end of the 1997-98 season.

Since then, Phil has been a regular member of United's team in the Worthington Cup matches, where he has had a chance to display his growing talent in midfield.

PHIL MULRYNE

JUNIOR MEMBERS

What would you give to sign for Manchester United? The cost of a chocolate bar a week, even the cost of a king size chocolate bar? If your answer's 'yes', then you could join thousands of others enjoying the sweet taste of success as United's junior members.

There are two membership packs to choose from:
Fred's Junior Devils and MU Youth.

JUNIOR DEVILS

As a Junior Devil you'll join up with Fred the Red, the cheekiest little devil in football and United's official 12th player. When you join, you get Fred's special welcome pack, filled with special Manchester United goodies:

EXCLUSIVE CUT-OUT MEMBER'S SHIRT

YOUR OWN MEMBERSHIP CARD (WITH SPACE FOR A PICTURE OF YOUR OWN FACE)

FRED'S OWN INSIDE STORIES

A MAGIC BADGE

RED, WHITE AND BLACK FACE PAINTS

FRED'S HAPPY/SAD FACE DIAL

A RED WHISTLE

A SIGNED CONTRACT FROM UNITED MANAGER, ALEX FERGUSON

And that's just the kick-off! During the year, you'll get two more mailings, including Fred's comic, packed with the little devil's top stories!

MU Youth

As a member of MU Youth you'll get your own:

MEMBERSHIP I.D.
MU YOUTH KEY RING
EXCLUSIVE PLAYERS TRUMP CARDS
A SIGNED CONTRACT FROM ALEX FERGUSON HIMSELF. WOW!

Hold on, though – there's more to come. You'll also get an organiser, which you can build into the ultimate MUFC book. There are two more mailings during the year, with more inserts to add to your collection, so that you can build up a detailed file on all there is to know about what makes United the world's greatest football club. Find out about: tactics, training, fitness and diet. Discover how United's stars played and trained their way to the top. Create your own database of club history. And learn all you can from the master himself – Alex Ferguson.

To find out about joining the Junior Devils or MU Youth, or both, write to:
Manchester United Membership Office,
Manchester United Football Club, Old Trafford, Manchester, M16 0RA.

The names of all the United players listed below can be traced out in the grid opposite. They read in a continuous line, going up and down, forwards and backwards, but not diagonally. Every letter in the grid is used; each is used once only. Use a pencil and a ruler to help you trace them out.

PETER SCHMEICHEL

DAVID BECKHAM	ERIK NEVLAND
GARY NEVILLE	PHIL NEVILLE
JESPER BLOMQVIST	MICHAEL CLEGG
ANDREW COLE	ALEX NOTMAN
JORDI CRUYFF	PHILIP MULRYNE
JOHN CURTIS	JONATHAN GREENING
PAUL SCHOLES	JAAP STAM
DENIS IRWIN	PAUL TEATHER
RONNY JOHNSEN	RONNIE WALLWORK
ROY KEANE	MARK WILSON
DWIGHT YORKE	DAVID MAY

U	Y	F	F	C	U	T	H	A	N	N	I	N
R	C	I	J	N	R	A	N	O	G	E	D	G
W	C	D	O	H	T	I	S	J	R	E	E	N
E	O	R	O	L	E	M	D	I	V	I	S	I
R	L	E	J	C	A	A	Y	D	A	R	O	N
D	G	G	E	L	H	H	P	E	N	W	R	N
N	A	D	I	V	C	I	L	E	A	I	N	Y
M	A	B	E	A	I	P	I	K	Y	O	R	J
J	H	K	C	D	M	M	U	L	R	E	N	O
E	B	L	I	S	T	G	E	N	Y	S	N	H
S	R	O	V	Y	R	A	O	T	N	P	E	R
P	E	M	Q	N	E	X	N	M	A	E	T	S
I	H	L	L	E	L	A	D	N	E	M	H	C
L	P	E	I	V	E	V	L	A	I	C	H	E
N	I	L	E	R	N	O	Y	T	H	L	U	L
E	V	L	E	I	K	R	K	E	G	S	A	P
O	R	A	R	I	L	N	D	W	I	C	H	O
W	K	M	K	W	S	O	T	L	U	P	A	L
L	W	E	N	O	E	H	E	P	A	S	A	E
L	A	I	N	R	R	T	A	M	A	T	J	S

FANTASTIC ART

Every week, Manchester United receive poems and artwork from supportive fans. Take a look at these arty pieces, then have a go yourself!

Ole Gunnar Sols by Jack Stalker (age 9)

This Year

The gang's all here,
The TV's on,
The dad's are all singing.
The Red's Victory song.
But don't let this fool you,
Dads are so uncool,
The team they support
Is mighty Liverpool!
But that success is history,
When standing was the game,
And terraces were for keeping fit,
Running up and down the same.
But now we live in '99,
This century's about to end,
It's Man United now,
That consistently sets
the trend.
Using speed and skill,
Whilst passing with care,
Collecting each season,
Yet more silverware.
But whatever our sport,
And wherever it's taught,
It's the kids in these teams,
Who've grown up with
these dreams.
So twelve years of growth,
Have made us tall,
Whilst watching Man U,
Dominate all,
And whilst United do succeed,
Soccer teams like ours,
Desperately need,
A Giggs or Beckham or
especially a Cole,
To help us score,
That winning goal.

But we don't have the money,
To buy and sell,
But we do have the heart,
To play so well.
We learn a lot from our heroes,
Whom we watch on TV,
Sadly, we can't get tickets,
For you or for me,
But to see a live game -
That is our aim!
For the first time to see,
And listen to the sound,
Of me and my team,
Enjoying the ground.
And to hear the supporters,
Creating a din,
As we all cheer,
Another United win!
So why should we go,
To watch this great team?
It would fulfil a 12 year old's dream.
It will inspire my generation,
Who till now has only seen,
Its heroes and exploits,
On the small screen.
And our voices will swell,
Milan's ground with our cheer,
As the Reds conquer Europe,
This year!

By Max Jones (Age 13)

David Beckham by Luke Chester

ANSWERS

OFF TO THE MATCH – PAGE 08

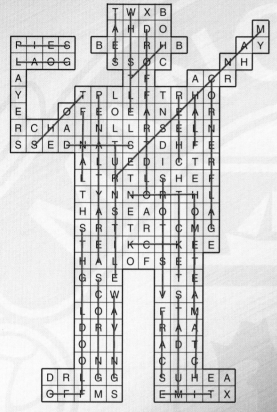

The left-over letters read: BOBBY CHARLTON CALLED IT THE THEATRE OF DREAMS.

TRAINING GROUND MAZE GAME – PAGE 22

CROSSWORD CHALLENGE – PAGE 18

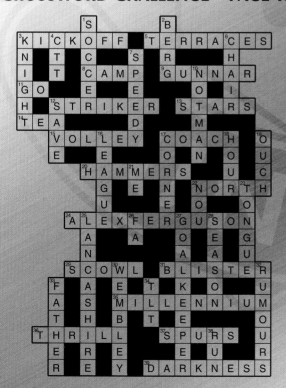

MIRRORED PICTURE PUZZLE – PAGE 30

ANSWER:3

ANSWERS

MINI QUIZ – PAGE 32

ALL AT 'C'
Answers:

1	Chelsea
2	Cole
3	Cruyff
4	Charlton
5	Cardiff
6	China
7	Cantona
8	Cork
9	Cricket
10	Champions

TAKEN AS RED
Answers:

1	predator
2	Fred
3	predecessor
4	incredible
5	Redknapp
6	shreds

BECK TO SCHOOL
Answers:

1	Andrew Cole (3 + 6 = 9)
2	Ryan Giggs (11 + 19 = 30)
3	David Beckham (12 + 7 = 19)
4	Ole Gunnar Solskjaer (20 − 16 = 4)
5	Henning Berg (7 x 3 = 21)
6	David Beckham (5 + 7 = 12)
7	David May (11 − 7 = 4)
8	David Beckham (21÷3 = 7)
9	Roy Keane (8 x 2 = 16)
10	Wes Brown, Gary Neville (30 ÷ 2 = 15)

ANYONE FOR SECONDS
Answers:

1	1996
2	European Cup Winners' Cup
3	David Beckham
4	Arsenal
5	Blackburn Rovers
6	Joseph
7	Henning Berg
8	1994
9	There hasn't been one
10	Oldham Athletic

THE ODD SQUAD – PAGE 44

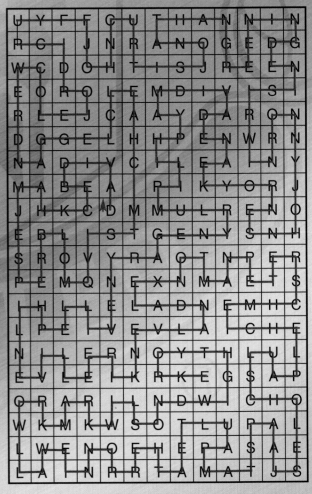

IT'S KNOT EASY – PAGE 50

ANSWER: A=3; B=5; C=1; D=6; E=2

SQUADDIES – PAGE 60